A ROOKIE BIOGRAPHY

MADAM C. J. WALKER

Pioneer Businesswoman

By Marlene Toby

Special thanks to A'Lelia Perry Bundles,
great-great granddaughter of
Madam C. J. Walker

◆P Children's Press ®
A Division of Grolier Publishing
New York   London   Hong Kong   Sydney
Danbury, Connecticut

Madam C. J. Walker (Sarah Breedlove) 1867-1919

Library of Congress Cataloging-in-Publication Data

Toby, Marlene.
   Madam C. J. Walker: pioneer businesswoman / by Marlene Toby.
      p. cm. — (A Rookie biography)
  Includes index.
  Summary: A biography of the Afro-American businesswoman whose invention of hair products led to great financial success.
  ISBN 0-516-04272-6
  1. Walker, C. J., Madam, 1867-1919—Juvenile literature 2. Afro-American women executives—Biography—Juvenile literature. 3. Women millionaires—United States—Biography—Juvenile literature. 4. Cosmetics industry—United States—History—Juvenile literature. [1. Walker, C. J., Madam, 1867-1919. 2. Businesswomen. 3. Afro-Americans — Biography. 4. Women-Biography. 5. Cosmetics industry — History.]
I. Title. II. Series: Toby, Marlene. Rookie biography.
HD9970.5.C672W3545 1995
338.7 ' 66855 ' 092 — dc20
[B]   95-7975
                                            CIP
                                            AC

Madam C. J. Walker was born
in 1867. She died in 1919.
She invented hair products
for African-American women.
She became a millionaire.
This is her story.

CONTENTS

Chapter 1

A Christmas Present

Madam C. J. Walker
was born Sarah Breedlove
on December 23, 1867.

She was a Christmas present
to her family — the only
present they got that year.
She was the first person in her
family to be born free.

Picking cotton was hard work. At the end of the day, workers were tired and sore. Sometimes their fingers would bleed.

Sarah's parents worked on a cotton plantation near Delta, Louisiana. So did her sister Louvenia and her brother Alex.

Until the Civil War, the Breedloves had been slaves. After 1865 they were free. But they were still very poor.

Children stayed close to their mothers as
they washed clothes in big tubs outside.

In the evening, she
worked in the family
garden, swept the yard,
and fed the chickens.

On Saturday, Sarah and
her mother and sister
did laundry for people.
They used big, wooden tubs.
Sarah liked to listen to her
mother sing as she washed.

When Sarah was seven years old, her parents died. They may have come down with a sickness called yellow fever.

For a while, Sarah, Alex, and Louvenia tried to keep up their farm work alone. Then Alex moved away to look for work.

Many people left their homes to get away from the disease of yellow fever. It was spread by mosquitoes.

Sarah Breedlove (Madam Walker) was born in this one-room cabin in Delta, Louisiana.

Sarah and Louvenia lived alone. They spent all their time washing clothes to make a living and keep their home.

Vicksburg, Mississippi, was a busy place in the 1870s. Steamboats and trains brought passengers and goods from big cities. They sent cotton to factories in New England and Europe.

But when Sarah was eleven, she and her sister lost their home.

They moved to Vicksburg,
Mississippi, to look for
work. Soon they were
washing clothes again.

In Vicksburg, Louvenia
got married. Sarah didn't
like Louvenia's husband.
She thought he was cruel.
She didn't like living
with them.

In 1882, Sarah got married,
too. She was fourteen years
old. She married Moses
McWilliams.

Chapter 2

The Mixture

Moses McWilliams wasn't a rich man. But he worked hard and so did Sarah.

When Sarah was seventeen, she gave birth to a baby girl. She and Moses named the baby A'Lelia. They wanted to make her life easier than their own.

When A'Lelia was only
two years old, Moses died
in an accident. That left
twenty-year-old Sarah
on her own.

"What can I do?" she
thought. She would not
go back and live with
Louvenia and her husband.

"Try St. Louis," said friends.
"You can make more money
washing clothes there."

So Sarah and A'Lelia
got on a riverboat
and headed north.

St. Louis was big and bright
and noisy. Sarah soon found
friends at her church and
settled down.

She still worked hard
washing clothes. But at
least she could send A'Lelia
to school. She even saved
money so A'Lelia could go
to college someday.

*Horse-drawn wagons loaded goods onto steamboats
in St. Louis. The picture on the opposite page shows
downtown St. Louis.*

Booker T. Washington (left) and his wife Margaret (below) were good leaders. They lived in Tuskegee, Alabama, but traveled a lot.

At the 1904 St. Louis
World's Fair, Sarah heard
Margaret Murray Washington
speak. She was the wife of
the great Booker T. Washington.

Sarah thought Margaret
Washington was a fine
lady. She wore a beautiful
dress, and her hair was perfect.
Sarah wished that she could
look like her.

Sarah was neat and clean.
But she had problems with
her hair. It was thin and
patchy. She tried putting
treatments on her hair.
But nothing seemed to help.

Then Sarah had an idea.
Why not make her own
mixture for her hair?
If it worked, she could sell
it and start her own business.

Sarah prayed for God's help.
Then she had a dream.
In the dream, a black man
told her what to put in her
hair mix.

After Sarah Breedlove started using her own hair treatment, her hair became soft and pretty.

Sarah made the mixture and put it on her hair. In a few weeks, her hair looked better. She asked her friends to try it. It made their hair look better, too.

That was all Sarah needed. No more laundry for her! She had a good hair treatment, and she would sell it. Now her own business was on its way.

Chapter 3

Birth of a Business

Sarah's brother Alex had
died in Denver, Colorado.
But his widow and daughters
still lived there.

So Sarah decided to start
her business in Colorado.
It would be good to be
close to her family now
that A'Lelia was away
at college.

In Denver, people could ride in horse-drawn carriages or automobiles. It was a busy place.

Sarah had only $1.50 when she came to Denver. She worked as a cook by day. She made her hair mixtures at night.

She called her three products
Wonderful Hair Grower,
Glossine, and Vegetable
Shampoo. The shampoo
cleaned hair. The grower
fought scalp diseases, and
the glossine softened curls.

Sarah Breedlove may have walked down city streets like these, selling her products door-to-door.

Sarah wanted her products
to treat the problem hair of
African-American women
and make it easier for
them to style their hair.

She began selling her products
door-to-door. Women loved
them. She also put ads
in newspapers.

But Sarah herself was
the best ad for her products,
because her hair looked
so good.

In 1906, Sarah married Charles Joseph Walker. He was a long-time friend from St. Louis. He moved to Denver.

This signature stamp was on many of Madam Walker's hair products.

From then on, Sarah called herself Madam C. J. Walker. She thought that name had style and would help her products sell.

Her products did sell well. Soon, Madam was traveling all the time. She sold her products and trained other women to sell them, too.

These women were called
agents. They went from
house to house treating
hair. They earned a good
living, and Madam sold
her products.

A'Lelia graduated from college
and helped run the mail-order
business in Denver. It grew
and grew.

But Madam thought she
would do even better if she
moved east. So she went to
Pittsburgh, Pennsylvania.

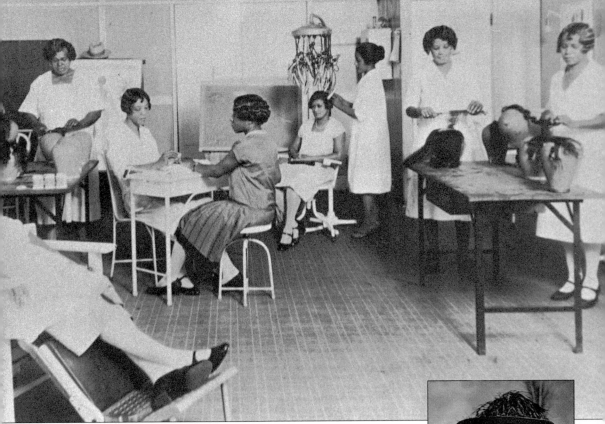

A'Lelia Walker (right) was in charge of the training school (above) where Madam Walker's agents learned how to use her products.

There she and A'Lelia opened a training school for Madam's agents. They called it Lelia College. The college gave many women jobs.

Chapter 4

Growing

Madam Walker spent two years in Pittsburgh. Then, in 1910, she left A'Lelia in charge and moved the headquarters to Indianapolis, Indiana.

She thought there would be more growth in Indianapolis.

Opposite page: Streetcars carried passengers up and down busy streets in Pittsburgh, Pennsylvania, in the late 1800s.

In 1911, Madam opened the Madam C. J. Walker Manufacturing Company in Indianapolis, Indiana.

Now that her business
was doing well, Madam
wanted to improve herself.
She studied penmanship,
letter writing, and public
speaking. She learned about
books, music, and art.

She owned many beautiful
things. She went on trips
in her expensive car.

Madam gave away
a good deal of money.
She liked to help people
improve their lives.

Madam Walker rode in this electric car. It was easy to drive and could go 30 miles an hour.

She spoke to many groups
about how she started her
business. She told them
how far she had come.
"You can do it, too," she said.

In 1912, Madam and C. J.
were divorced. That same
year, A'Lelia adopted a young
girl, Mae Bryant. Madam
was now a grandmother.

Madam was very busy
traveling. In 1913, she took
her products to Central
America and the Caribbean
Islands. Soon she had even
more agents.

East 112th Street in Harlem (right). The Walkers lived in a four-story town house on 136th Street. Lelia College and the Walker Hair Parlor were in the same building. At least twenty women graduated from the college every six weeks.

She began spending much
of her time in New York City.
In a place called Harlem,
there were many black businesses.

It was a place for artists and
entertainers and politics, too.
She liked the lively place.
She moved there in 1916.

Chapter 5

"To Help My Race"

Madam Walker's business helped many black women improve their lives. Some were hired to help run the business. But most were her agents.

In 1917, Madam brought together all her agents. She held the first meeting in Philadelphia.

Madam Walker's business went on even after her
death. Walker Beauty School graduates (above)
got together in St. Louis in the 1930s.

Madam showed them how
to sell more products.
She gave prizes to those
who did the most good
in their communities.

Madam Walker's life was
very full. She had her
business, her family and the
people she helped, and her
work for civil rights.

She also had her home—
a mansion on the Hudson
River in New York that
she had a black architect
build for her.

Madam almost never rested.
"You must rest," said her
doctor. "Your blood pressure
is too high."

*Madam Walker's mansion near the Hudson
River in New York was called Villa Lewaro.
It had thirty rooms in it.*

Madam Walker spent very little time resting at home. She was busy doing things for other people and showing them how to make life better for themselves. This made her happy.

Madam Walker was too busy to rest. She was with friends in St. Louis when she became very ill. She returned home to New York. However, she only grew worse.

"I want to live to help my race," were her last words. Madam C. J. Walker died on May 25, 1919. She was 51 years old.

She was a millionaire when she died. And her last words had come true. She had helped her race. During her life she gave people jobs and money. She helped women feel good about themselves and take pride in their work.

Most of all, she helped others see what one poor black orphan girl could do. Madam C. J. Walker's life said to others, "I did it. So can you!"

Important Dates

1867   December 23 — Born in Delta, Louisiana,
to Minerva and Owen Breedlove

1874   Parents died

1882   Married Moses McWilliams

1885   Daughter A'Lelia born

1887   Moved to St. Louis, Missouri

1905   Moved to Denver, Colorado, and started
her business

1906   Married Charles Joseph Walker

1908   Moved to Pittsburgh, Pennsylvania

1910   Moved to Indianapolis, Indiana

1916   Moved to New York City

1917   Began Hair Culturists Union for Walker agents

1918   Had mansion built along Hudson River,
New York

1919   May 25 — Died at Irvington-on-Hudson,
New York

Index

Page numbers in boldface type indicate illustrations.